CATS

Lesley Anne Ivory

BARNES
&NOBLE
BOOKS
NEW YORK

The best are such as are of a fair and large kind,
and of an exquisite tabby colour.

William Salmon

☆☆☆☆☆

A Chinese legend tells how the cat originated
from a cross between a lion and a monkey.
From the lion came dignity, strength,
courage and grace. From the monkey
came curiosity and playfulness.

Traditional

But the kitten, how she starts,
Crouches, stretches, paws and darts!
William Wordsworth

*****

I soon realised the name Pouncer in no way did
justice to her aerial skills. By the end of the first
day, I had amended her name to Kamikaze.
Cleveland Amory

*****

It always gives me a shiver when I see a cat
seeing what I can't see.
Eleanor Farjeon

There are no ordinary cats.

Colette

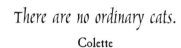

＊＊＊＊＊

Most cats, when they are Out want to be In,
and vice-versa, and often simultaneously.

Louis J. Camuti

＊＊＊＊＊

Cats are not people. It's important to stress that,
because excessive cat watching often leads to
the delusion that cats are people.

Dan Greenburg

Webster was very large and very black
and very composed. He conveyed the impression
of being a cat of deep reserves.

P.G. Wodehouse

✶✶✶✶✶

Cruel, but composed and bland,
Dumb, inscrutable and grand,
So Tiberius might have sat
Had Tiberius been a cat.

Matthew Arnold

No matter how much cats fight,
there always seem to be plenty of kittens.
Abraham Lincoln

*****

She would come home in a shocking state,
all bedraggled, her fur so torn and dirty
that she had to spend a whole week
licking herself clean. After that, she would
resume her supercilious airs ...
and one fine morning, she would be found
with a litter of kittens.
Émile Zola

It is a very inconvenient habit of kittens
(Alice had once made the remark) that,
whatever you say to them, they always purr.

Lewis Carroll

✫✫✫✫✫

Cats do not bother with ... control games.
They are simply in control of their own lives,
period. If they walk away from you,
it is because they have got better things to do.

Steve Duno: The Everything Cat Book

To respect the cat is the beginning of
the aesthetic sense.

Erasmus Darwin

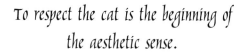

✫✫✫✫✫

There are two means of refuge
from the miseries of life: music and cats.

Albert Schweitzer

✫✫✫✫✫

Cats are a mysterious kind of folk.
There is more passing in their minds
than we are aware of.

Sir Walter Scott

How comes Kitty acts not like the beast of prey
she is, but like a better-class human being?
I don't know the answer.
The point is she does it—and
makes you her slave ever after.

Paul Gallico

✫✫✫✫✫

As a cat lover, you will know how much
positive emotion is generated by your pet.
Amazingly enough, that "warm glow"
of affection you both feel when she is curled up
on your lap ... is a very real force of energy.

Alison Daniels: Feng Shui for You and Your Cat

A home without a cat,
and a well-fed, well-petted and properly
revered cat, may be a perfect home, perhaps,
but how can it prove its title?

Mark Twain

＊＊＊＊＊

A cat can be trusted to purr
when she is pleased, which is more than
can be said for human beings.

Dean Inge

The smallest feline is a masterpiece.
Leonardo da Vinci

✶✶✶✶✶

The really great thing about cats is
their endless variety. One can pick a cat to fit
almost any kind of decor, colour scheme, income,
personality, mood. But under the fur,
whatever colour it may be, there still lies,
essentially unchanged, one of the world's free souls.
Eric Gurney

✶✶✶✶✶

The cat is a dilettante in fur.
Theophile Gautier

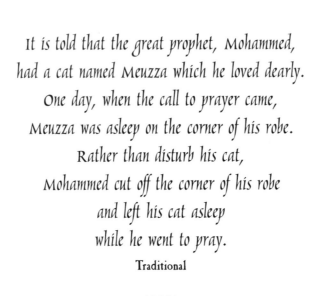

It is told that the great prophet, Mohammed,
had a cat named Meuzza which he loved dearly.
One day, when the call to prayer came,
Meuzza was asleep on the corner of his robe.
Rather than disturb his cat,
Mohammed cut off the corner of his robe
and left his cat asleep
while he went to pray.

Traditional

✦✦✦✦✦

If man could be crossed with the cat, it would
improve the man but deteriorate the cat.

Mark Twain

People who belong to Siamese cats must
make up their minds to do a great deal
of waiting upon them.

Compton Mackenzie

*****

Of all domestic animals, the cat is the most
expressive. His face is capable of showing
a wide range of expressions.
His tail is a mirror of his mind.
His gracefulness is only surpassed by his agility.
and, along with all of these,
he has a sense of humour.

Walter Chandoha

Of all animals, he alone attains the
Contemplative Life. He regards the wheel of
existence from within, like the Buddha.

Andrew Lang

✫✫✫✫✫

A little drowsing cat is
an image of perfect beatitude.

Champfleury

✫✫✫✫✫

A cat sleeps fat, yet walks thin.

Fred Schwab

I value in the cat the independent and almost
ungrateful spirit which prevents her attaching
herself to anyone ... When we caress her,
she stretches herself, and arches her back
responsively. But that is because she feels
a pleasant sensation, not because she
takes a silly satisfaction in faithfully loving
a thankless master as the dog does.

Chateaubriand

✵ ✵ ✵ ✵ ✵

Cats, like men, are flatterers.

William S. Landor

Cats seem to go on the principle
that it never does any harm
to ask for what you want.
Joseph Wood Krutch

*****

When a cat looks at you and then half closes
its eyes, it's not ignoring you.
The animal is telling you that
it's relaxed in your presence.
Michael W. Fox

Lesley Anne Ivory's paintings

This edition published by
Barnes & Noble, Inc., by arrangement with
Michael O'Mara Books Ltd,
9 Lion Yard, Tremadoc Road,
London SW4 7NQ

2001 Barnes & Noble Books

© 2001 Michael O'Mara Books Ltd

Illustrations © Lesley Anne Ivory 2001
Licensed by ©opyrights Group

M 10 9 8 7 6 5 4 3 2 1

ISBN 0-7607-2594-2

Design: Mitchell/Strange
Printed in Singapore by Tien Wah Press